my

SECRET IS

SILENCE

☽

poetry and sayings of

ADYASHANTI

OPEN GATE PUBLISHING

Los Gatos, California

Acknowledgments

A heartfelt thanks to Prema Maja Rode for all her tireless work, inspiration and dedication to making this book a reality.
Deepest gratitude to our "Rumi-reciting friend," Eric Raymond Schniender whose poetic eye, editorial expertise and generous offerings of time and talent were invaluable in the creation of this book.
Additional thanks to the following people who contributed their heartfelt service to this project:

Annie Gray, Liz Siverts, Steve Kurtz, Hamsa Hilker, Diane Kaye, Susan Kurtz, Pernilla Lillarose, Kamala Kadley, Elaine Kreston, Pam Montanaro, Tom Kirby, Robin Rose, Liz Rose, Marjorie Bair, Elizabeth Orr, Gary Wolf and Priya Irene Baker.

ISBN: 0-9717036-1-2

Cover design courtesy of Liz Siverts
Cover photos courtesy of Steve Kurtz
Photo of Adyashanti courtesy of Diane Kaye

For more information, contact:
Open Gate Publishing*
P.O. Box 782
Los Gatos, CA 95031, USA
www.zen-satsang.org

*Open Gate Publishing is a division of Open Gate Sangha, Inc.

To my wife, Annie—
a soft and shining benediction
and the object of my secret devotion.

Contents

Foreword

I first met Adyashanti several years ago at a gathering in the mountains of Santa Cruz, California. Apart from a lit candle and a small Buddha statue with a sword, the room was unadorned. He was young, American, married, head shaven, and dressed in western clothing. He spoke with gentleness and humor on the subject of awakening to the truth of who we really are—Divinity itself.

There is always a conspicuous and refreshing absence of esoteric terminology and spiritual jargon in Adyashanti's teachings. While occasionally quoting Buddhist or Christian texts to highlight a point, Adyashanti does not espouse any ideology, theology or religion. He speaks from the immediacy and authority of his own experience. Like the teas he enjoys mixing, Adya blends Zen, inquiry, and who-knows-what-else into his own dharmic brew.

Adyashanti seems to be living simultaneously from a permanent residence in the eternal and a vacation home here on earth—in a body, fully functional, fully human. There is a celebration of existence, a complete welcoming of shadow and light, and always a pointing to the emptiness, the silence, beyond and within all form.

During that dharma talk in Santa Cruz, Adya spoke about *embodiment*, how the realized self dances in the "function and activity" of human experience. In the course of the day, I shared an awakening experience that had become a distant memory. "How do I get back there?" I asked.

Adya's response was that it is impossible to get back there. He explained that it was an experience of enlightenment, and enlightenment is not an experience. If it comes and goes, he said, that's not it. He then invited me to notice the ever-present awakeness looking out through my eyes in that very moment. I instantly saw that my busy, lifelong search for an authentic awakening obscured the simple fact that everyone is already, unavoidably, awake.

That day and in many encounters since, I have been touched by Adya's genuine humility, his humanity and the laser-like precision and subtlety of his guidance. I have seen time after time the remarkable way Adya meets each questioner with openness, without agenda, never putting himself higher or lower, never forcing or judging, just allowing the unfolding of whatever wants to happen. Adya is a master gardener gently nurturing any sprouts of awakeness, delighting when someone blossoms in the truth. A wonderful community of truth-lovers gathered around him makes a most inviting and lovely garden.

The collection of poetry and sayings in *My Secret is Silence* offers invitations to inquire, to awaken, and to celebrate the beautiful gift of existence. Culled from journals, talks, and dialogues with students, it is remarkable how many ways Adya can point to silence, to the unseen, to nothingness. He is a lively flame that never dances the same way twice. Toward the purpose of waking the mystery to itself, Adya will caress you, tickle you, play with you, threaten you, use a flamethrower or a sword, or just love you to death…whatever it takes. "This is a *results* game," he says. With a wink and a smile Adya informs us, "I am not trying to give you a spiritual experience. I just want to cut off your head."

I study and recite the poems of the Sufi mystics Jelalludin Rumi and Hafiz, and now have a new mystic poet in my repertoire. Adya's poetry has a Zen-like elegance and directness without being stark or cold. Like Hafiz' poetry, it is infused with sweet intimacy, playfulness and the homeyness of a dear old friend. It also contains Rumi's wildness and fierce clarity. With Adya we visit the tavern, gaze lovingly at the moon, or experience the ranting threats of the spiritual arsonist. But where Rumi and Hafiz often whirl, bewildered in ecstatic bliss, Adya's expression is simple, immediate and grounded in the everyday: a kiss, the gesture of an open hand, hearing a bird, watching cooks in the kitchen, sipping tea. The button from a marine's coat reveals "all of mankind's violence and its will to live and love."

Freedom and ease always inform Adyashanti's poetry and teachings as they spontaneously emerge, unlabored, from the emptiness. Some poems are the mystery looking inward, trying to describe itself, able only to speak the strange tongue of opposites and that which lies beyond. Some share observations and hints, then inquire: "What do you really want?" or "What is the shape of love?" A spiritual question "like a weight on the end of a fishing line…takes you in, in, in." Words can only refer to an object, to some*thing*, and can't begin to portray that which doesn't exist. They are simply too noisy. Adya gestures eloquently beyond words to their silent source:

The Friend's Heart beats
Do you hear it?
It is your own.
It sounds like this . . .

As Adya says "We are just putting words to things that are wordless. Words aren't where it's at."
Words simply do not have the capacity to contain or express the majesty of this constantly moving, multi-dimensional, full-sensory, holographic show called reality. They are only a pretty flyer, an invitation with directions to the main event: YOU are the show, always playing now. Don't miss it!

Love and blessings,

Eric Schneider
January 2003

Introduction

Did you see the moon in the sky?
"Yes," I said.
With a tear of knowingness
in her eye, she said:
That's why we are all here, to see the moon.

~ Adyashanti

My Secret is Silence is like a moon reflecting light
from an unseen sun. When viewed through the clear
and empty window of your open mind and heart,
each saying, each poem, each chapter in it reflects
the radiant light of your own Being.

When reading this collection, it may be useful to
remember that no single expression, if taken by itself,
can represent the whole. When Adyashanti gives a
talk, also known as *satsang* (association with Truth),
he often reminds his students that Truth cannot be
contained within the conceptual framework of words.
So read with your heart, not just your mind. Take in
fully what rings true for you and set the rest aside for
the moment.

Each chapter of this book highlights a theme that
follows a general movement of the spiritual journey
that begins with the spiritual search and culminates
in the dance of true non-duality. Each poem is
followed by sayings that serve to further illuminate its
message.

In the first chapter, "A Tendency to Shine," Adya
speaks to and about the spiritual seeker. He invites
you to "wake up" from your conceptual dream-world,

to look beyond the ideas and beliefs that cause suffering, and to discover the radiant light of awareness peering through your own eyes in this very moment. You *are* what you have always been looking for. *You* are the love that you have always wanted.

In the next chapter, "Enlightenment Is a Gamble," Adyashanti explores the process of surrender. He addresses spiritual seekers who have touched upon the Love that "demands everything," but who have not yet given themselves fully to it. This is the most demanding of the chapters, while also being the most fun. Here Adya shares, in no uncertain terms, what price one must pay in order to live what is realized. He urges you to put it all on the line and "for once in your life," lose your final hand to God.

The more you lose, the more Love "replaces you," and the more its demand becomes an invitation that you willingly accept. In Chapter 3, "The Shape of Love," Adyashanti speaks about Love and the call to live and move as Love embodied in form:

Drink the wine of this Love
and your life will change.
Instead of being a gatherer
of the Divine Light
you will be its shine.

It will be the end of you
and the beginning.

In the next chapter,"Laughing Buddha," we see a specific example of how Love moves in the world, in the form of Adyashanti himself. Here Adyashanti shares his personal perspective and experience of living as Silence dancing in form. The first poem offers a glimpse into his experience of final awakening: "I heard a bird one day and became the bird hearing." Adya introduces this chapter with a suggestion about how to read it: "I am a window. Look through me, not at me." There is no need to look toward Adyashanti as a reference of how to think or behave. The true teacher is simply an empty space through which we can view the world beyond the wall of our conceptual mind.

The final chapter, "The Eternal Song" offers the perspective where there is no distinction between personal and transpersonal, no separation of self and other. If you read this chapter with your thinking mind, it may not make sense. Rather, listen with your whole being, from the place where all perspectives dissolve and dance together, where there is no particular point of view. How do we do this? Adyashanti suggests, "Rest and be taken."

The Epilogue, "Only Awareness Remains," is a prose summary of the journey contained in this book.

As you embark upon this precious journey in *My Secret Is Silence*, prepare to lose everything. In exchange for all the knowledge and familiar identities you thought were keeping you safe, you will realize the sweetness of living in total surrender to that which you have always loved. As Adyashanti has said, "I am not so much a spiritual teacher as a thief. Stick around here, and you will lose your most cherished illusions. Be forewarned, this wondrous journey will not be anything like you imagined it would be."

Enjoy this book. Allow it to open you, challenge you, delight and inspire you. Let yourself in on Adyashanti's "secret" that the empty window of Silence is everywhere and always revealing the infinite forms of your own beauty.

May you bask in the reflected light of your own true Self.

Prema Maja Rode, Editor
December 2002

My Secret Is Silence

A Tendency to Shine

☽

Because of an innocent misunderstanding you think that you are a human being in the relative world seeking the experience of oneness, but actually you are the One expressing itself as the experience of being a human being.

A Tendency To Shine

If you prefer smoke over fire
then get up now and leave.
For I do not intend to perfume
your mind's clothing
with more sooty knowledge.
No, I have something else in mind.

Today I hold a flame in my left hand
and a sword in my right.
There will be no damage control today.

For God is in a mood
to plunder your riches and
fling you nakedly
into such breathtaking poverty
that all that will be left of you
will be a tendency to shine.

So don't just sit around this flame
choking on your mind.
For this is no campfire song
to mindlessly mantra yourself to sleep with.

Jump now into the space
between thoughts
and exit this dream
before I burn the damn place down.

If you want to wake up, the first thing you need to seriously consider is that you are asleep and everything you take as real is a dream.

☾

Cease cherishing beliefs. If you could follow this one simple instruction to its absolute conclusion, you would be enlightened, free, truth-realized.

☾

God doesn't play by the rules.

DEAR JOURNEYER

Have you made love to empty
and soulless things for too long?
I know that you get a little crazy
when you have not paid attention
to the Heart inside your heart
and like a man in the desert
dying of thirst
you see things
that aren't really there.

If your heart is thirsty for Love and God
then turn around now and
go back to where you came from
back to the simple ground of your origin
inside the inside of this
flowering and Radiant Emptiness.

*When we start to suffer, it tells us something
very valuable. It means that we are not seeing
the truth, and we are not relating from the truth.
It's a beautiful pointer . . . it never fails.*

☾

*Your intrinsic nature is still as pure and clear
as it was before you ever took this birth.
If you would just turn your attention away from
the various trance-inducing states created
by your mind and realize the intrinsically
innocent and pure nature of the unseen seer,
you would at once experience a great relief
and freedom.*

☾

*Put attention on what is alive
with freshness and vitality.
Do not put attention on what is dead,
repetitious or dull.*

COME TO YOUR SENSES

There is only one Truth
and as you go looking for it
through a forest of seeking
be careful lest you bump into a tree.
That lump on your head
may remind you that
everything is God.

You are like a forest dweller
looking for the forest.
What am I to do?

Listen friend
each crackling leaf beneath your feet
is a personal invitation
to come to your senses.

Has it ever occurred to you
that you are seeking God
with His eyes?

Stop looking from your cloud of hazy thoughts.

Looking from that vantage point is pure folly.

Look from behind that cloud of thinking.

There it is always clear.

☾

It is the same awareness that is looking
through your eyes right now.
It's not a different awareness.
It's not a special awareness.
It's the awareness that always is.

☾

Just for a moment,
don't try to go from point A to point B.
Let yourself just be here.
Let yourself stop becoming more,
or better, or different.

I WOKE UP LAUGHING

I had a dream last night.
We were all inside the sacred temple
looking for the entrance.

Who would have thought
that such insanity exits in heaven?
At first light I woke up
laughing.

The joke of it all is that you are looking from
your true nature right now without knowing it.
If you would stop being fascinated
with the contents of your mind,
you would experience what I am saying.
Feel your way into what I am saying
rather than thinking about it.

☾

Only a self-concept looks and longs for God.
Drop your self-concept and there is only
God meeting God.

☾

Enlightenment is the restoration
of cosmic humor.

WHY I TEACH

I am sitting with my
brothers and sisters
lovers and friends.
Words fall from
this empty mouth
into the clean air
thrown like seeds
onto the fertile ground.
The core is waiting
to be opened and exposed
eaten and digested.

I am talking to you
dear one
yes you
the hidden one.
Your stomach is empty and hungry.
I know well the pain of deprivation
the mouth that cannot swallow
the parched throat that cannot drink.

I am talking to you.
I have not forgotten you
I am there beside you.
I have seeds to eat
and sweet milk to drink.
But you must take them.

You need not chew or swallow.
You can take my offering
directly into the Heart.
Let it burst open wide and
throw stars across space.

I will wait for you
my brother
my sister
my lover
my friend.
I was sent for you
to expose you to yourself.

You are not a walking mistake.

You are not a problem to be solved.

☾

Let go of willfulness
and rest in willingness.

☾

Wanting to get away from
the pain fuels everything.

☾

In expecting self-realization to be
something special, you miss it.

God is not in the clouds, but under your feet.

I WILL NOT WHISPER

I want to speak to you about Love
about how you deny yourself
its slightest entry
about how much you truly fear
Love's silent embrace.

I want to talk to you
about what you will not
allow yourself to see—
about that beauty inside
that you turn your face from.

Yes, I want to talk to you.
You who have somehow
found a way to hide
within a sliver of darkness
cast upon the pure light of Being.

I want to talk to you.
I will not whisper.

You can live in that sliver of darkness forever
and tell yourself lies.
You can blame yourself.
You can blame others.
You can blame God and beyond.
And still that Love that you are will wait

until you can tell yourself
the lie of denial no more.

And at that very moment
you will see
just how silent Love's embrace can be.
And in that silence
the truth will ring clear.
Love demands everything:
all of your illusions
excuses and fears.

I want to speak to you about Love.
I want to talk to you about
what you will not allow
yourself to be.

I want to talk to you.
I will not whisper.

We suffer in the present from past experiences
in direct proportion to how much identity
we derive from that suffering.

☾

The easiest way to keep dreaming
is thinking your dreaming is true.

☾

Don't get mixed up with the "whys,"
they will not help you.

☾

Whatever you resist you become.
If you resist anger, you are always angry.
If you resist sadness, you are always sad.
If you resist suffering, you are always suffering.
If you resist confusion, you are always confused.
We think that we resist certain states because
they are there, but actually
they are there because we resist them.

ON RECEIVING KEN'S MARINE COAT BUTTON

He put life and death into my hand.
He gave me cold fear
and warm relief.
He gave me a piece of his past
and a piece of his present.
He gave me all of mankind's violence
and its will to live and love.
He gave me a piece of his honor
and his trust.

I have a gift in return
a gift that cannot be given.
I have an empty
outstretched hand
and in the darkness
he will grope for it blind
and on his hands and knees.

In a quiet moment
he will find it.
And in that finding
he will find himself.
His hand will be empty too.

All cruelty arises from beliefs.

In the absence of all belief, love shines.

☾

We are no more dangerous than when we are

trying to impose heaven upon earth.

☾

The true awareness shines from the heart

not from the head.

☾

Before you start to meditate, ask yourself a question:

Is it true that peace and silence are not here now?

With our intention to move towards quietness,

the first step we take is away from it

because we assume it's not here already.

THE SPIRITUAL MASTER

When you come upon him
you will know him by the way
he steals everything sacred
from the palm of your hand.
Others will promise you more.
He will promise you nothing
not even one damn miracle.

You will trick yourself with
his teachings.
You will listen to each word
that falls from his lips in anticipation.
But while he speaks
his eyes are laughing.
You will record his words
and listen to them.
Read them over and over
looking for the secret meaning.

But his true voice will elude you
because *you are looking for*
and not listening.
You are looking for
and not listening.
You are looking for
and not listening.

*As a spiritual teacher, my job is to express
something that can't be expressed.
My job is to fail well.*

((

*Don't imitate your teacher or your guru.
Find within yourself that power which moves him.*

((

*The problem is that most people seek out
religions of all sorts as a way to relieve themselves
of the burden of finding and verifying the truth
for themselves—as if they could ride piggy-back
to enlightenment on the shoulders of some religion
or what some enlightened guy in the past said.*

((

*Don't get hooked on me, I'm very addictive.
I should have come with one of those
warning labels on my forehead.*

Wake Up!

So you have tasted that drug
called a spiritual experience.
And now you want more.

Like any good junkie
you will give anything for your drug
and most likely you have.
When you do not have your drug
you feel the sting of withdrawal
from the pit of your stomach
to the racing
anxious thoughts
in your head.

How much would you give
to have another hit of transcendence
course through your entire being
bringing with it such sweet euphoria
and an ever deepening addiction?

If God would only mainline
non-ending transcendence
into your veins
you would never suffer withdrawal.
This is the hidden hope
of all spiritual junkies.

Here is the Truth:
The Truth is not an experience
or an idea
the Truth is that
you have been dreaming.
Wake Up!

There is no one to be enlightened or
unenlightened.

It's the fear of taking a swan dive into the void
that is ultimately the cause of all this nonsense.

☾

I am not trying to give you a spiritual experience.
I just want to cut off your head.

☾

A spiritual question is like
an alarm clock thrown into the dream.
"Who Am I?" calls into question
everything the dreamer believes in,
namely him or herself.
It disrupts the dream. That's its purpose.
When your alarm clock goes off in the morning,
its purpose is not to get an answer.
Its purpose is to wake you up.

☾

*This is **not** dreamland spirituality.*

THE KISS

Isn't it time to stop loving and hating the mirages
of your virtual reality mind?
Time to slip like space
into the radiance of your bright and
Imageless Face.

Let it kiss itself in recognition
of its own beauty
and you will spend the rest of your life
loving all the various ways you shine.

Quick now, tell me something of God . . .
and not one word of it from your mind or you
will lose your life again.

☾

When the mind ceases all imagination
there arises a crystalline truth so real and concrete
that all the world seems dreamlike in comparison.

☾

There is only life living itself,
life seeing itself,
life hearing itself, life meeting itself
as each moment.

Enlightenment Is
A Gamble

☾

You can't follow a spiritual path like a lemming to enlightenment. It simply doesn't work that way. An unwillingness to question every step of the way will stop you dead in your tracks. The path to enlightenment is strewn with those who have chosen to take a position or an identity along the way. And the closer you get to enlightenment the more dead bodies you will be stepping over until finally you step right out of yourself and arrive at the goal, exactly where you have always been. Except now there is no one standing there.

MY SECRET IS SILENCE

The waves of mind
demand so much of Silence.
But She does not talk back
does not give answers nor arguments.
She is the hidden author of every thought
every feeling
every moment.

Silence.

She speaks only one word.
And that word is this very existence.
No name you give Her
touches Her
captures Her.
No understanding
can embrace Her.

Mind throws itself at Silence
demanding to be let in.
But no mind can enter into
Her radiant darkness
Her pure and smiling
nothingness.

The mind hurls itself
into sacred questions.

But Silence remains
unmoved by the tantrums.
She asks only for nothing.

Nothing.

But you won't give it to Her
because it is the last coin
in your pocket.
And you would rather
give her your demands than
your sacred and empty hands.

To surrender willfulness and positionality
is the greatest act and the doorway to
infinite love and freedom.

☾

As long as you mistakenly look to the mind
for truth, it will continue to haunt you to no end.
The best course of action is to look
and see for yourself that nothing in the mind
is ultimately true, real or existing.

☾

What seems so real to you
is only imagination to me.

☾

The question actually leads you into silence.

HOUSE OF CARDS

The host of this house of cards
is silently watching
the drunken madness
of the guest called me and you.

There is no greater addiction
than to being me.
That great drunken fool
who only knows how to stumble on along
speaking drool-lipped nonsense to himself.
Five hundred drunken lifetimes
is enough
for even the most persistent fool
to begin to see his folly.

This house is not for the
knowledgeable ones
for they are too drunk
to know that they are fools.
This house is a fool's house.
For only those who are truly foolish
will find themselves to have
drunkenly stumbled
this far astray from insanity.

Has it ever occurred to you that it's
not happening anywhere outside your head?

☾

Fathom this: There is nothing to grasp.
*You have been **it** all along.*

☾

Life is always and constantly the invitation
to find out what's true, to unlock every illusion.
And you only know you've gotten
to the bottom of it is when the illusion is gone.

What Do You Really Want?

Let your brain whirl and spin itself
into blessed exhausted silence.
Let it rest like a baby
in the open palmed hands
of the heart held Now.

What do you really want after all?
To win, to pick the sweetest fruit on the tree?
Or to rest from the endless succession
of temporal moments
and the promises that they never keep?

What do you really want?
To take or be taken?
To find the Great Pearl of liberation
or to be consumed by it?

Seek only to die into yourself.

☾

There is a presence that is unnamable
which thought cannot touch.
It is not your possession; it is what you are.

☾

Just jump in.

☾

Don't try to hold onto what is realized,
be what is realized. You cannot maintain
realization or sustain it. In order for it
to always be, you must be it yourself—
in your humanity.

☾

Truth replaces you. It takes up residency.

How Empty Is Your Cup?

Sitting in this tavern all day long
is not for the weak of heart.
The abundant wine flows rich
into the empty glasses only.
Whether you are thirsty or not
does not matter.

How empty is your cup?
is all the wine maid asks.
How empty is your cup?

The wine maid said
I have heard the occasional stranger
protest this request by saying:
"But I am the work hand
who watered the vines
and harvested the grapes
under the hot sun
working day in and day out
for little pay and even less relief
from this harsh life."

To such lost souls
the wine maid smiles a little and asks:
Why do you drink such sour wine?
Is pride really worth such a bitter taste?

Empty your cup and I will fill it
with your heart's desire.

Those who make it to this tavern
are the lucky ones.
Why sit in heaven and complain
about the road taken?
All the Winemaker wants
is to quench your thirst
to fill empty cups
over and over again.

Besides, I asked Him once
if He would mix old wines with new.
He just began to laugh.
That was my first day on the job—
more years ago than I can count.
And He's still laughing
and I am still pouring His wine.

Everybody has their favorite way
of arguing with God.

☾

When you start to follow, instead of lead,
you start to follow that inner movement that
is not speaking. It leads; you follow.
Eventually the leading and following
are just one movement.
There is really no leading, no following.

☾

You must choose between
your attachments and happiness.

☾

This idea that there is a problem…that's the
wild hair in the ass of humanity.

COME OUT TO PLAY

What is God?
A living contradiction
perfectly resolved within itself.
That's why God makes you so crazy
and shines with the only sanity there is.

Best to cash in all your arguments
and come out to play in the
empty field.

Everything is a spark of that eternal radiance.

Why flee from the world in order to find it

when you yourself are already on fire?

☾

Come to satsang to perceive what is real,

not to solve what is unreal.

☾

The nature of Source is expression.

☾

If this isn't making any sense to you, don't worry,

it will some day.

ENLIGHTENMENT IS A GAMBLE

Time to cash in your chips
put your ideas and beliefs on the table.
See who has the bigger hand
you or the Mystery that pervades you.

Time to scrape the mind's shit
off your shoes
undo the laces
that hold your prison together
and dangle your toes into emptiness.

Once you've put everything
on the table
once all of your currency is gone
and your pockets are full of air
all you've got left to gamble with
is yourself.

Go ahead, climb up onto the velvet top
of the highest stakes table.
Place yourself as the bet.
Look God in the eyes
and finally
for once in your life
lose.

There is no such thing as "fake it 'til you make it"
in the enlightenment business. It is all about truth.
No faking allowed, no consolation prizes.

☾

This is a results game.

☾

It's about as much fun as you can have
while being burned at the stake.

☾

I am here to take away your illusions –
your illusions of control, of freedom, of self.
You think you have control but you don't.
You think you have freedom, but you don't.
You think you have a self, but you don't.

☾

I'm not one of those spiritual comfy guys.
I'm one of those spiritual alarm clocks.

THIS WINE IS WITHIN YOU

This tavern is about to close its doors.
So my friends, we must go.
But do not rejoice
or regret your leaving
for this Wine is within you
the warm nectar of
a thousand Buddhas.

We will meet together again at this tavern
I am sure
but do not forget
that at the innermost table
this Wine of ours is always flowing
and it is where all true lovers dwell.

Within the stillness of Stillness
you will be met there
and consumed by the Winemaker
by the object of your secret devotion.
Then you will sing
the most drunken song of all:
I am He, you will sing
I am She, you will sing—

the song of your long awaited
return to your senses.

The true Self is the direct experience
that no-self exists.

☾

As long as there is a body there will be the
me sense. But you stand prior to the me sense.
Although it is there, you are prior to it, as I.

☾

Selflessness arises out of the realization that
you are the world and much more as well.
All arises within you and is an expression of you.

THE END OF VAJRAPANI RETREAT

I have given all that I am
as have you.
Whether wearied or exalted
let's fall on the floor laughing.

What a colossal blunder
we have all fallen prey to,
slipping into sanity like this.

Our minds are surely gone
when we see everything as God.
Prepare yourself Mother Earth
the inmates are loose
the fools have
broken free of their chains.

There is no such thing as integrating truth into an illusion.

☾

The spiritual rubber hits the road when truth begins to act within this human existence.

☾

There is no future in this.

The Shape of Love

(

It is one thing to come upon enlightenment, the breaking through distinctions to the great unity. It is quite another to realize its function and activity. Until the emptiness can dance spontaneously, realization is not complete.

THE INNERMOST TABLE

You want me to speak of love
and so I will.
But the Love of which I can speak
costs me all my coins of illusion
and so I cannot compromise its virtues
nor quibble over its price.

This Love is Divine Nectar
a wine found only at
the innermost table.
It has seen endless days
of rain and sun and harvest.
It has been made wise and mellow
by the passing of time
and its refined taste
is uncompromising to those
who prefer their wine young
and overly sweet.

Although at times you may
appear to be swept away
by its dizzying effects
you will find that you have
the clarity of a diamond and
the reflexes of a falcon.
You will remain capable of compassion
and ruthless decisiveness alike.

In one hand
you will hold a feather
and in the other
a sword.

Drink the wine of this Love
and your life will change.
Instead of being a gatherer
of the Divine Light
you will be its shine.

It will be the end of you
and the beginning.

A total acceptance of yourself brings about
a total transcendence of yourself.

☾

Wisdom without love is like having lungs
but no air to breathe. Do not seek wisdom in order
to acquire knowledge but in order to
live and love more fully.

☾

No person or event has the power
to make you happy or unhappy.

PRAISE THIS DAY

Save your mentally manufactured tales of
enlightenment-to-come for someone else's ears.
The price to enter this love
is your hope for a better future.

We are not a crowd of beggars here.
You and I have been down that long, twisted road
all the way to its end.
Here we do not ask God for favors
but instead celebrate the light in each other's eyes.

So if you are ready to stop denying yourself
your own beauty
you have come to the right place.
Wake up now and praise this day
when you realize that God's eyes
are the ones you are looking out of, and into.

Praise this day—
and with each breath you take
be filled with the golden arc of love
which announces the ending of
your argument with God.

Praise this day
simply because it exists
and sit down now in the warm skin

of your own lap;
for you are home
and it is time to rest
in the merciful light
of your own eyes.

*Spiritual love is the expression of
an undivided self.*

☾

*Don't forget that you are the clear
light of awareness.*

☾

*There is nothing but the One
in relationship with itself.*

BE DONE WITH IT

I commend my Spirit
unto the grace of the Great Way.
Whether consciously or not
this has always been
the doorway to liberation.

All you lovers of truth
and all you true lovers
now is the time to be done with it.
Wash your battle-scarred hands
in this Presence among us.

Cast off your warriors' clothing
and slip into your night slippers.
Untie your hair or cut it off.
The Hidden One is present
and doesn't care where you've been
or what you've done
or what you are doing now.

Commend all of yourself—
body, mind and spirit
to this Grace.
Slip out into the night air
into the waiting

quivering birth of this
Golden Heart.

Lean down now
like wet, green grass and
kiss the bottoms of your feet.

There is something deeper than pain and pleasure:
wanting to know what is true.

☾

Just for a moment, take your hands
off the steering wheel.

☾

Here is a secret: The Buddha has never
been born, nor has the Buddha ever
been absent from birth, life or death.

☾

At each moment we are expressing what
we know ourselves to be. If we know ourselves
very little we will express and manifest
that unconsciousness of our true nature.
If we know who and what we are very thoroughly,
we will express and manifest that in what we do.
It is all very simple.

MEET ME HERE

Join me here Now
where there are no points of view.
Slip under good and bad
right and wrong
worthy and unworthy
sinner and saint.

Meet me here
where everything is unframed
before understanding
and not understanding.

Meet me here
where silence roars
where stillness is dancing
where the eternal is living and dying.

Meet me here
where you are not you
where you are It
and It is unspeakable.

Meet me here
where all points of view
merge into a single point
that then disappears.

Meet me here
before there ever was something
before there ever was nothing.

Meet me here
where everything speaks of this
where everything has
always spoken this
where nothing is ever lost or found.

Meet me here.

This is it right now!

☾

You cannot think about reality
nor can you imagine it with images in your head.
When you are caught within a dream, the
only way to be free is to wake up from that dream.

☾

Don't look outside of change for the changeless.
*Change **is** the changeless. If it did not change*
you would not know that the changeless
is here at all.

☾

Never oppose anything or anyone.
Instead, choose to express and manifest
what is true for you.

YOUR SWEET DEVOTION
for Eric

My Rumi-reciting friend
you are becoming the object
of your sweet devotion.
You drip with the same honey
that sweetened
Rumi and Hafiz's poems.

My friend
you are the honey
inside this honeycomb existence.
From your bright nothingness
comes the taste of God.

Yes, I know you have your
moments of doubt.
But each one brings you closer
to the doubtless.
So throw caution to the wind
and dare to love
even the bee's sting.

Whatever you see, taste, touch, hear or smell is
a product of your own creativity. You are
the One experiencing itself.

☾

You can never know when you are at the last layer,
until all of a sudden it's revealed and — poof,
the house of cards collapses. You've gone through
the bottom, and the sense of inadequacy no
longer has the power to draw you back out of
your true nature.

☾

You can't find it, neither can you lose it.

☾

The illusion of self is an operational necessity.

The Calling

I heard You call,
answered and became the calling.
I thought I wanted love
but instead became the loving.
How was I to know
that desire awakens and
becomes the desired?

This mind no longer holds beliefs—
some other power moves it. I call it love.

((

It is not so much the joy of being loved
as it is the joy of loving and being love itself.

((

Don't try to find yourself or define yourself
through what you do; instead, seek only
to express your highest knowing of what you are
through what you do.

((

By being nothing you are everything.
By wanting nothing you are eternally full of grace.

THE SHAPE OF LOVE

What we see is not the most important.

Could dust rise without the invisible
hand of the wind?
Could a fan turn without any current?
Could lungs breathe without breath?
Tell me
What is the shape of Love?
How much does Joy weigh
when held in the palm of your hand?
Can you catch the Spirit of Life in a jar?

All things seen depend
upon the Unseen.
All sounds depend
upon Silence.
All things felt depend
upon what is not felt.

God is always dancing—always.

☾

*Consciousness at rest is experienced as
formless being or aware space.
Consciousness in motion is experienced
as all forms, as life or existence itself.*

☾

*There is only God's will, even if it is
to fight against God's will.*

IT SOUNDS LIKE THIS

You live not by your own hand
but depend entirely upon
the unseen Friend.
Your truest face has no form.
The Friend's Heart beats.

Do you hear it?
It is your own.
It sounds like this . . .

You cannot find it because you are it.

☾

*Whatever the image of yourself, it's a mask
and it's hiding emptiness.*

☾

*This isn't a battle against the mind.
Eventually the mind realizes that it just wants
to be in adoration of a truth and a wisdom
that it cannot contain.*

SACRAMENT

Sometimes I touch your face
knowing that it is God.
The light in your eyes
a soft and shining benediction.
People think of you in various ways
but I know who you are.

Form is a sacrament
and the formless its benediction.

☽

Where awareness and love meet as one,
that is the home of wisdom and liberation.

☽

Where all concepts disappear is the place
where we are much closer to the truth.

KOBUN

Great dharma-cloud Kobun
has passed through the empty sky.
A lifetime of raining Buddha wisdom down
onto patch-robed monks.

Today his dharma rain is a tear in my eye.
A moment of sadness touches
what is tender inside.
Daughter and father pass away together
in the space where tragedy and love meet.

Note: Kobun Chino Otogawa Roshi, the much-beloved founder of Jikoji and
other Zen centers, drowned while attempting to save his six-year old daughter,
Maya, who also drowned in Switzerland on July 26, 2002.

You are neither free nor bound, but ever-present.

☾

There is only God's business
because only God is.

☾

Unspeakable doesn't mean big.
It just means unspeakable.

Laughing Buddha

☾

I am a window.
Look through me
not at me.

I HEARD A BIRD ONE DAY

Wind moves through
this hollow reed body
touches the five senses
and becomes a song.

Who is the Master
of this orchestra
and how does Emptiness
become love or a teacup?

I heard a bird one day
and became the bird hearing.
Then waking from this spiritual dream
of Oneness
the world resolved itself
and nothing at all happened.
Yet the Ancient One continues to
wink and smile.

Awareness woke up

out of being fused with form.

☾

The fictitious me is an accumulation from the past.
*All that has been accumulated becomes the **me** sense.*
Only by dispelling this accumulation
does the sacred present itself.

☾

It is not the joy of attaining a state
but the joy of utter relief
from the struggling and the seeking.

☾

The absolute truth includes duality.

LAUGHING BUDDHA

When I broke open
Buddha broke open.
And neither of us
has been the same since.
In an instant
we fell into each other laughing
and neither one of us survived.

But still the sun shines in the morning
and sets in the evening.

I am like a friendly old dog now
wearing my master's night slippers.
Yet somehow
they fit perfectly.

Find enlightenment, then let it go.
Become a sage, then step out of her clothing.
No one will know you ever again.

☾

This world is not my concern; it is myself.

☾

From this Oneness, individuality can be celebrated.

☾

An ordinary man seeks freedom
through enlightenment.
An enlightened man expresses freedom
through being ordinary.

CURIOUS HANGOVER

When I lost myself
I lost my God too.
Like a collapsing tent
everything fell to the ground.
Now there is nothing to contain
the space inside of things
nor keep the space outside out.

How was I to know
that finding meant losing
and losing meant finding?

When the world rights itself
in your eyes it is like waking
from an intoxicating dream
with a curious hangover
that chuckles in bewilderment saying
What was that all about?

There is only one thing going on.

☽

The miracle isn't that some people
wake up out of this dream,
the miracle is that people don't.

☽

Your eye is God's eye.

☽

You think that enlightenment is something
other than what is happening right now.
This is your primary mistake.

I HAVE COME HERE

I have come here
into this life
not of my own will
but of the will
of the Hidden One—
the One who sprouts every seed
the One who causes the leaves to fall
the One who beats hearts
and breathes air into lungs.

I have come here
as a spark cast off
of the Eternal Fire
looking for dry grass
and a gentle breeze
to kindle the Hidden One's
heat into flame.

This light that I am is no ordinary light.
It does not light up anything
or illuminate darkness.
It is a pure and formless knowingness.

☾

I am the source and its servant.

☾

People don't need my comfort; they need reality.
Reality is its own comfort.

☾

Truth comes to an innocent mind as a blessing
and a sacrament. Truth is a holy thing
because it liberates thought from itself and
illumines the human heart from the inside out.

FALL RETREAT

The two cooks deliver sweet fruit
and crunchy nuts
to my room every day.
It is their offering
so I pick it up
and I eat it for Buddha.
Some days I am hungry
and I eat it all.
Some days I am not hungry
and I still eat it all.
I eat it all
because that is how the Buddha
receives their offering.
That is how Buddha digests
the cooks' love.
Love needs to be offered
received and digested.
This is enlightened activity.

When I eat the sweet fruit
I am sweet
Buddha is sweet.
When I eat the crunchy nuts
I am crunchy
Buddha is crunchy.
When I am hungry
this is Buddha's enlightenment manifesting.

When I am not hungry
this is Buddha's enlightenment manifesting.

I know a secret:
the cooks are Buddhas
feeding Buddhas.
I saw one of them
dancing in the kitchen today.
The other was laughing.
There is a vow of silence here
which everyone has broken
whether they have spoken or not.
But these two laughing
and dancing cooks
have not broken the vow once.

If you understand this
through and through
your mind is pure.
If you do not fully comprehend it
you are a beggar
with gold in his pockets.

Here I offer Buddha's enlightenment
and maybe you'll receive it
but still you must digest it fully.
You must digest yourself fully

until there is no more indigestion.
Then you become an offering.
You become sweet fruit
and crunchy nuts
dancing.

*Very often our first dharmic relationship is with
our spiritual teacher. Dharma means truth.
In that relationship I am not committed to your
happiness, I am not committed to your well-being.
I am committed to the truth within you.*

☾

The true emptiness is smiling.

☾

*I am not trying to get you to experience
what I experience, but to realize what I realize.
Your realization will have its own unique
experiential tones which will not be exactly
the same as mine, nor anyone else's.
The realization is one;
experiences differ and change.*

TEA TASTING

I like to sip sweet tea
a mix of peppermint and licorice—
amber gold and smooth as silk.
I have a silk shirt
that feels like that tea tastes.
It sits on my shoulders
like a warm breeze.
That tea tastes like Ramana's soft eyes
like Buddha's serene face.

People go looking far and wide
For the Buddha's enlightenment
but I just sip my tea
and my tea swallows me.

The Buddha breaks into a grin
and Ramana winks one eye
like my grandfather did
when he knew that I knew
what he knew.

I like green tea too.
Strong and bitter
like the taste of grass.
Like tasting sure defeat—
the kind that you can
taste on the tip of your tongue

the kind that can change
your life on a dime
forever.
With each bitter sip
Manjushri's sword
cuts the mind to pieces
cuts it awake
and cuts awakeness
into emptiness.

People come here
and listen to my dharma words
when all I really want to do
is sell them a little tea.

Unlike the modern day view of Zen as a bunch of
Buddhists who like to rake rocks into interesting
patterns and come up with cute, unsolvable riddles,
the real aim of Zen is enlightenment.
Zen is about waking up, freedom, and liberation.
All the rest is just window dressing and shackles.

☾

Dealing with the linchpin that holds it all
together—that's what I am interested in.

☾

First you are a seeker, then you are a finder.
Then, you are what you were before you were
a seeker and a finder.

There You Go Again

Ever since I stepped out of imagination
and into the heart of things
I have become so much less spiritual.
Heaven, hell and earth
hold no meaning for me anymore.
For I am neither coming
nor going
nor staying put.
All I do is notice all the various ways
that Light weaves itself into dreams.

When someone asks me who they are
or what God is
I smile inside and whisper to the Light:
There you go again pretending.

Everything came from nothing.
Nothingness came from what I am.

☾

Thought is creative. It creates everything.
The most creative thought is the originating
thought, the very first thought. In the beginning
was the "word" and the word was made flesh.

☾

Don't look to make good decisions or
the best decision or even the right decision.
Make the decision that best expresses and
manifests who and what you know yourself to be.

So Cheap

I am all hollowed out now
like a reed.
I gave everything for this.
And still I laughingly wonder:
How could it have been so cheap?

Every time you try to turn around and
look for yourself, you don't find anything.
Because you are without form.

☽

The known is least true.
The unknown is more true.
That state which is prior
to knowing and not knowing
is the truth itself.

☽

The plot twist changes. But underlying that,
something is the same, and as far back
as you can remember.

BORN TO AWAKEN MYSELF

I was born to awaken myself
over there
playing the part of you.

I join with you and
we realize together
as One Being
the truth eternal.

This world is my dream,
and it speaks myself back to me.
I meet myself over there as you, he, she, they, it.

☾

It's a psychological revolution that comes
simply from seeing what is. It's like holding
a match to a dry leaf and the leaf catching on fire.
That's what seeing Truth does.

☾

Don't sit around and have a party
about what just revealed itself.
Get on with it.

☾

Don't talk to me about the real and the unreal,
illusion and enlightenment. When you
come upon the truth it silences all
categories of thought.

The Eternal Song

☽

All spiritual experiences are to be eventually left behind. One day even your awakening to enlightenment will be seen as a flash of imagination which served only to orient you toward your own disappearance into simplicity and the restoration of cosmic humor.

Annie's Hazy Moon of Enlightenment

Did you see the moon in the sky?
"Yes," I said.
With a tear of knowingness
in her eye, she said:
That's why we are all here—
to see the moon.

Existence is pure love.

It is totally in love with itself.

☾

Because the One is nothingness,

all things are created by it.

Because the One is pure potential without form,

all forms spring forth from it and celebrate it.

☾

Total stillness of being comes when

all resistance to movement is absent.

When all resistance is absent,

there is complete stillness, an alive stillness,

a vital stillness which is pure movement

without resistance.

HAVE YOU NOTICED?

I have no more ideas anymore about
God, consciousness,
the absolute or non-duality.
If you want to talk with me
let us meet where
there are no abstractions.

All I want to know is:
Have you noticed?
Something is here
my friend.
Something is here
have you noticed?

Only the Mystery is.
The Mystery is noticing that
only the Mystery Is.

Have you noticed?

Consciousness always yields itself back to illusion.
It's always coming back to meet every illusion
because if it doesn't wake the illusions up,
Emptiness can't dance.

☾

There is all this talk about whether there is
free will or no free will,
but such talk misses the mark.
*For **whom** is there free will or no free will?*

☾

All conceptual understanding is a form
of fundamentalism.

☾

It amazes me that they ever got around to making
religions, theologies and theories out of this.

Rest and Be Taken

When there is deep abidance
there is nowhere to abide.
There is nowhere to rest
or grasp onto
and yet there is rest.

The sky abides
yet it never rests.
Neither can we say that
the sky is not always at rest.
We talk about the sky
as if it were something
as if it actually exists—
and yet we cannot say that
the sky does not exist.
The sky is nothing but
coming and going.

Everything is perfectly spontaneous.
The coming and the going arise mutually
instantaneously.
If the true I is asleep
you will miss the point entirely
and you will continue to dwell
in the world of opposites.

So see the two as one
and the one as empty
and be liberated
within the world of duality.

At first it seems
as if begoing follows becoming.
But look even closer
and you will see
that there are only
flashes of lightning
illuminating the empty sky.

Life and death
becoming and begoing
are only words.
In order to save your life
you must see that you die
instantaneously
moment to moment
instant to instant.

Now where are you going to abide?
And where are you not abiding already?

Indeed there is nowhere
to rest your head

and there is nothing but rest.
So let go of all ideas
about permanence and impermanence
about cause and effect
and about no cause and no effect.
All such notions are dualistic concepts.

The Truth of what you are
is completely beyond all duality
and all notions of non-duality,
and yet it includes duality
and non-duality alike.
Like an ocean
that is both waves and stillness
and yet un-definable
as waves or stillness.

The truth of being
cannot be grasped by ideas
or experiences.
Both waves and stillness
are the manifest activity
of your own self.
But self cannot be defined
by its activity
nor by its non-activity.
The truth is
all-transcendent

ungraspable, all-inclusive
and closer than your own skin.

A single thought about it
obscures its essence.
The perfume of true life
is right in your nose.
There is nothing you can do
to perceive it
and yet you must do something.
I say:
Rest and be taken.
Rest and be taken.

No words can penetrate here.

☽

There is an intimacy that is there
before the first word is spoken.

☽

Never define yourself, and you will see
that everything everywhere
is an extension of yourself.

☽

When thought enters into the changeless
it goes silent. When thought goes silent,
the thinker, the psychological me,
the image-produced self, disappears.
Suddenly it is gone. You, as an idea, are gone.
Awareness remains alone.

WHO ARE YOU?

You Are…
beyond the body, mind and personality
beyond all experience and the experiencer thereof—
beyond the world and its perceiver
beyond existence and its absence
beyond all assertions and denials.

Be still and awaken to the realization
of who you Are.

In this realization of no separate self
the Supreme Reality which you Are
shines unobscured
in all things, as all things, and beyond all things.

Having returned to the formless Source
and transcended all separateness
do not stop or cling even to this Source
but go beyond to the Supreme Realization
which transcends all dualities
yet does not deny even a speck of dust.

The enlightened sage abides
as the eternal witness
wholly unconcerned, yet intimately engaged.
Resting beyond all definitions
he neither clings to transcendent freedom

nor is he entangled by the dualistic world;
therefore, he is at one with all of life.

Living in the perfect trust of Supreme Realization
he has nothing to gain or lose
and naturally manifests love, wisdom
and compassion—
without any personal sense of being
the doer of deeds.

Having abandoned all concepts and ideas
the enlightened sage lives
as ever-present consciousness
manifested and manifesting
in the world of time and space
That which is eternal, ever new, and whole.

In this unobscured realization
Supreme Reality shines consciously
in all things, as all things, and beyond all things.
Shining unobscured, it penetrates
the entire universe.
Penetrating the entire universe
it knows itself as Self.

The true I is I-less while remaining as I.

☾

All of existence
is none other than myself
and yet I transcend all of existence
and all of myself.

☾

You can neither look for the truth,
nor find the truth, nor lose the truth;
for all the time you are the truth.

ITSELF

The unseen
is seeing itself.

The unfelt
is feeling itself.

The unknown
is knowing itself.

The unspoken
is speaking itself.

The unmanifest
is manifesting itself.

Emptiness knows itself by flowering.
If emptiness did not flower,
it could not know itself.
Flowering and knowing are one and the same.

☾

Whatever you bring to love turns to flame,
leaving only sacred ash behind.

☾

If you are lucid within this dream,
your experience of it is totally different
than if you're not.

☾

Stop looking to your experiences
to validate your realization.
No experience validates the realization of truth.

NOTHING IS HAPPENING

Some touch upon the perception
that nothing ever happened.
But few perceive that nothing
is happening Now.

It is all a movie
a projection
by consciousness onto consciousness.
But really nothing is happening.
Nothing is ever really happening.
It only appears that way.

So within nothing happening
something is happening
but whatever is happening
is not really happening
although it is happening.

If you understand these foolish words
you can be said to be enlightened.

When your mind collapses inward and falls into
the void, and when the void falls into itself,
there is no return. It is finished.

☾

In <u>The Tibetan Book of the Dead</u>...
every one of those "bardo states" that they
talk about existing after you die
actually exists here and now.
You are in a bardo state.
It's called the human experience.

☾

I gave birth to God, not the other way around.

Emptiness Dancing

When I rest in my origin
I am the unmoving cause of all movement.
With no will nor intention of my own
all things move forth from my own being and
express my unspeakable and unknowable self.

Although I never move away
from my unmovable nature
all movement is my own.
Although I am the unmanifest and inexpressible
all manifestation in all the worlds are
expressions of my infinite creative potential.

I am always at rest
and wildly dreaming this moment
into and out of existence.

When I return

to my true and ultimate origin,

there is no I who returns

nor origin to return to.

☾

To live in truth is to be newly born at each instant.

☾

Why does the world exist?

Because emptiness dances, because it is wild,

because it endlessly gives birth.

Before God Was God

In my complete nature
there is neither I nor God.
Here, I am what I have always been
before I was I, or God was God.

Here, I remain as the uncreated and uncaused.
All things emanate from
and have their cause in
this causeless ground
in this fertile emptiness
in this which is neither dark nor light.
No eye has ever gazed upon this—
only from it.

What I am is without identity.

☾

Birth is when I appear out of myself.
Life is when I dance within myself.
Death is when I disappear into myself.

☾

You may say my teaching is confusing
because I am not consistent. But I say,
"Does a flame ever leap up from the fire
exactly the same way twice?"
The radiance of truth and life
does not fit into conceptual pockets.
It is always leaping out in celebration of itself.

THE ETERNAL SONG

I Am the aware presence.
Everything in existence
is an expression of what I Am.
I Am the clearness in the sky
the infinite in space
the wetness in water
the sweetness in sugar.

In what I Am there is no knowledge
of what I Am.
I Am beyond the knowledge
of what I Am.
Both the known and the unknown
are expressions of what I Am.

I Am the seeker and the sought
the finding and the losing
the silence and the sound.

I Am the joy within happiness
the tears within sorrow
the presence within stillness
the awareness within sleep.

Both illusion and enlightenment
bondage and freedom
heaven and earth

exist within what I Am.
In what I most essentially Am,
I Am dissolves into
what I have always been.
I Am the awareness of each moment
the consciousness of all content
the presence within all things.

I Am the stability within mountains
the heat within fire
the intimacy within love.
In realizing what I Am
I come to peace within myself.
Realizing that I Am not hidden
but ever present
I come to rest within myself.

Realizing that what I Am
cannot be gained nor lost
I naturally stop seeking
for what I already Am.
Realizing that all forms
are expressions of myself
a great and silent love
perfumes each moment.

I Am the faceless
wearing all faces.

I Am the stillness within movement
and the movement within stillness.
I Am the emptiness within all forms
and the fullness within emptiness.
I Am here and now
everything
and nothingness too.

When we realize who we are, we no longer have
this endless confusion, this eternal battle with
ourselves. Therefore we tend to not struggle
with others or the world.

☾

Consciousness comes back for itself, all of itself.
It is never satisfied just to transcend illusion;
it always comes back to liberate illusion.

☾

Freedom is the absence of the seeker of states.

☾

You just become a living invitation.

ONE SPRING BREEZE

One spring breeze
ten thousand leaves fall.

☾

When emptiness is still, that is eternity.

When it moves, that is love.

☾

ENDLESS BENEDICTION

This flame of living Truth:
movement without division
action free of doubt
thought without thinking
wisdom born of the unknown.

This endless benediction
birthing itself from the origin of all
never leaving or forsaking itself
timelessly present always
shamelessly displaying itself
as *This*, right here
never leaving any trace
behind.

On the razor's edge between birth and death,

there is a fire. The leaping of that flame

is living truth.

☾

When you finally arrive at the true Oneness,

not even the Oneness remains;

neither is it absent.

☾

Actualizing has to do with translating

enlightened vision into human activity

without succumbing to ideas, ideals

or images of perfection.

☾

Since everything is already

the supreme Buddha Nature,

where are you going to go to find it?

Epilogue

☾

Life moves, undulates, breathes in and out, contracting and expanding. This is its nature, the nature of what is. Whatever is, is on the move. Nothing remains the same for very long.

The mind wants everything to stop so that it can get its foothold, find its position, so it can figure out how to control life. Through the pursuit of material things, knowledge, ideas, beliefs, opinions, emotional states, spiritual states, and relationships, the mind seeks to find a secure position from which to operate.

The mind seeks to nail life down and get it to stop moving and changing. When this doesn't work, the mind begins to seek the changeless, the eternal, something that doesn't move. But the mind of thought is itself an expression of life's movement and so must always be in movement itself. When there is thought, that thought is always moving and changing.

Actually, there is no such thing as thought, there is only thinking. So thought which is always moving (as thinking) cannot apprehend the changeless. When thought enters into the changeless it goes silent. When thought goes silent, the thinker, the psychological "me," the image-produced self, disappears. Suddenly it is gone. You, as an idea, are gone. Awareness remains alone.

There is no one who is aware. Awareness *itself* is itself. You are now no longer the thought, nor the thinker, nor someone who is aware. Only awareness remains, as itself. Then, within awareness, thought moves. Within the changeless, change happens. Now awareness expresses itself. Awareness is always expressing itself: as life, as change, as thought, feelings, bodies, humans, plants, trees, cars, etc. Awareness yields to itself, to its inherent creativity, to its expression in form, in order to experience itself.

The changeless is changing. The eternal is living and dying. The formless is form. The form is formless. This is nothing the mind could have ever imagined.

There is, quite literally, nothing to understand.

For more information about satsangs, weekend intensives and retreats with Adyashanti, or to purchase books and live recordings of Adyashanti's talks, please visit our website, or write to us and request a copy of our current newsletter.

www.zen-satsang.org

Open Gate Publishing
P.O. Box 782
Los Gatos, California 95031 USA